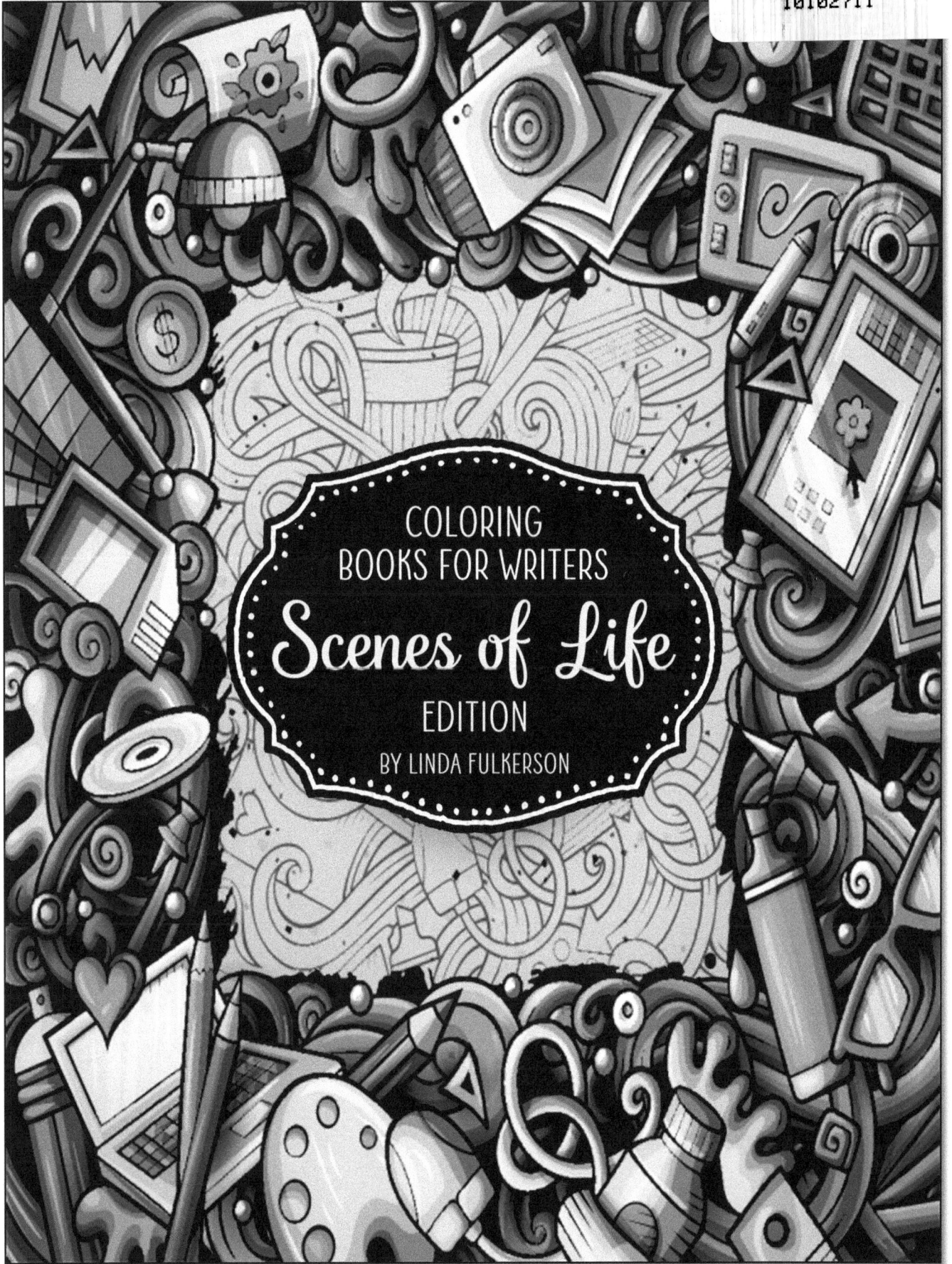

COLORING
BOOKS FOR WRITERS

Scenes of Life

EDITION

BY LINDA FULKERSON

COLORING BOOKS FOR WRITERS
SCENES OF LIFE EDITION

By Linda Fulkerson

www.LindaFulkerson.com

Ideas to Books
Morrilton, Arkansas

Coloring Books for Writers: Scenes of Life Edition
Copyright ©2018 by Linda Fulkerson.

For information about the author visit:
LindaFulkerson.com

Ideas to Books – Publishing Division
Morrilton, Arkansas

Book and Cover design by Book Marketing Graphics
www.BookMarketingGraphics.com

Cover images and internal illustrations were purchased through a licensing agreement.

ISBN: 978-0-9725092-3-7

First Edition: January 2018

INCLUDES:

Coloring Pages
and
Story Starters with Brainstorming Helps

BRAINSTORMING YOUR STORY

Start by asking yourself, "What if . . . ?" and brainstorm answers to that question.

During your "what if?" time, try to come up with the following story elements:

- Who? Who is your main character – your hero/heroine (also called the Protagonist)?
- What? What situation does the main character find himself in (story problem)?
- Why? What is his goal, and why does he want it? This is the story objective.
- Why not? What conflict is preventing your protagonist from attaining his goal? This is the story opponent or antagonist.
- How does it end? This is the outcome or climax.

WRITING YOUR STORY'S PREMISE

Once you come up with those items, you can write a two-sentence summary or story premise. Here's an example from my murder mystery, DEAD BROKE, using the SPOOC technique[1] (Situation, Protagonist, Objective, Opponent, and Climax) taught by creative writing instructor and author, Deborah Chester:

(Situation) When her brother is framed for murder,
(Protagonist) sports photographer Andrea Warren
(Objective) returns to the hometown she renounced to prove his innocence.
But can she clear her brother's name when
(Opponent) the true murderer
(Climax) discovers she's on his trail and determines to kill her, too?

After you've written your premise, the next step is brainstorming scene ideas that develop your premise further. Make a list of scenes you'll need in your story and start brainstorming what will take place in those scenes.

You can use the space in this book to record your thoughts, or use my Scene Worksheet (download link in the next section) and print off as many copies as you need. When you're finished brainstorming a scene, you can place that scene's worksheet in a folder/binder or scan the worksheet and save it to your computer. You could also type your notes into a word processor or a writer's organization program, such as Scrivener, which is what I use and recommend. If you prefer writing your ideas by hand, you can get a notebook to record your story starter/scene ideas.

---

[1] For detailed information about this technique, I recommend that you read *The Fantasy Fiction Formula* by Deborah Chester.

ELEMENTS OF SCENES

A fiction story is a simply cohesive collection of sequences called scenes. A scene is simply a part of the story where characters, or a character, engage in some sort of action, with or without dialogue. Once you've come up with a premise, scenes are the story blocks that connect the protagonist's initial situation with the story's climax.

Like the novel itself, each scene must have a beginning, middle, and an ending. It's a mini-story, if you will. An effective scene is written in the point of view (POV) of one character, and that character will have a goal he or she hopes to accomplish during the scene. The character should have a strong motivation as to why it's important that he accomplishes his goal in the scene. This is the "Why?" or the "Or else" factor. The reader must understand how important reaching this goal is to the character and what consequences will follow if he fails.

In addition to the point of view character and the scene goal, scenes include a specific setting – a where and when. Scenes should also contain some sort of conflict that challenges the character's achievement of his or her scene goal. The struggle against the conflict will result in growth of your character.

Finally, a scene concludes in an outcome, an answer to the underlying (and typically unwritten) question, "Will the point of view character attain his/her scene goal?" In his book, *Techniques of the Selling Writer*, Dwight Swain discusses scene outcomes. He explains there are basically four outcomes to a scene:

- Yes
- No
- Yes, but . . .
- No, and furthermore . . .

A simply "yes" to the story question would be boring. Even a no, while disappointing, will still bore the reader. Readers read to gain an emotional experience by identifying with and cheering for the story's hero and/or heroine. "Yes" and "no" answers don't build emotional tension.

So, if you grant their wish (scene goal, creating a consequence (Yes, but . . .), the story's tension increases, and the reader keeps reading to see what will happen next.

A good example of a "Yes, but . . ." answer to a character's goal can be found in The Little Mermaid. Ariel visits the sea witch and requests a set of legs. Her motivation for wanting legs is that she's fallen in love with a human. Does she get her legs? Yes, *but* it costs her one of her greatest assets – her voice. This setback immediately sparks a worry in the reader's brain – will Ariel get her voice back? The reader keeps reading to find out.

For the "No, and furthermore . . ." outcome, imagine your character has a scene goal to win a car race. As the he rounds the last curve and approaches the finish line, leading the pack, the scene question "Will he win?" seems to be an almost certain, "Yes!" But, at the last possible second, a tire blows, sending the hero's vehicle tumbling into the wall. Did he win the race? No. *And furthermore*, his car now needs expensive repairs, plus he suffered serious injuries. Yikes!

The character's motivation can be used to deepen the emotional tension. For instance, in our race driver example, what if the hero desperately needs the prize money because his ailing mother is about to lose her life-long home due to medical bills? Now, he has not only lost the opportunity to catch up her mortgage payments, but the wrecked racecar adds even more financial stress to the family. It's hard to be mean to our characters, but it keeps the reader reading.

When the character faces disaster in the scene outcome, she will react. That reaction can be as quick as a sigh of frustration or as complex as several pages of description about her resolve to try, try again. The disaster often leaves a character facing a dilemma of what to do next.

In *Gone with the Wind*, Scarlett O'Hara searches her farm for food and finds a lone radish. She faces a dilemma – starvation is a real possibility. She must make a decision: give up and starve or fight. Scarlett's reaction to disaster/dilemma/decision is portrayed in a powerful scene of her thrusting a fist toward heaven and declaring, "As God is my witness, I'll never be hungry again." That vow motivates her actions for the rest of the story.

Good writers use scene structure to keep readers turning the page by ending each scene with a hook, or cliff hanger. This is accomplished by saving the character's reaction to the scene outcome (yes, but . . . or no, and furthermore . . .) until the next chapter, ending the chapter with the disastrous outcome. The reaction, while necessary, is often anti-climactic. Ending a chapter at the worst possible moment for the character hooks the reader into turning the page.

Of course, not all reactions will be reflective. If the scene disaster leads the character to react with anger or plans of revenge, go ahead and show her loading her gun and storming out the door before your chapter ends. Whether the reaction segment is reflective or suspenseful, it should set up the next scene.

I've developed a scene worksheet, which you can download and print for use during your scene planning. It provides space to jot down notes about the elements your scene will need: POV Character, Other Characters, When/Where, Scene Summary, Character Goal/Scene Question, Character Motivation, Conflict, Disaster (Scene Outcome), Reaction, Dilemma resulting from the Disaster, Decision, Hook, and a space to list items to research. You can download a copy from my website by going to this link: www.lindafulkerson.com/free-scene-worksheet.

HOW TO USE THIS BOOK

With a little imagination, even seemingly everyday (a.k.a. boring) settings/situations can be developed into a fascinating story. The Story Starter topics in this book are, for the most part, all normal, everyday parts of our lives. Have some fun by coming up with interesting story concepts for everyday scenes of life.

You can use this book in whatever way helps you brainstorm story ideas, but the following steps are a suggested method:

Step One: Brainstorm "what if?" ideas while you color each topic's coloring page. Come up with a "What if?" question that will be the overall problem your story's hero will face.

Step Two: Develop that story question into a premise, using the Premise Formula form included with each Story Starter topic. Write your two-sentence premise for each story starter.

Step Three: Use the scene worksheet (shown on the next page) to brainstorm a scene that supports your premise and write that scene. Here's that download link again in case you missed it in the previous section: www.lindafulkerson.com/free-scene-worksheet

Step Four: Use the Story Notes area to jot down any ideas that you may have about a potential story on the topic you're brainstorming about.

Step Five: If you wish to continue developing this story, make a list of all scenes needed to complete your story, and then repeat step two until you've written all your story scenes. Organize your scene notes in either a binder, a notebook, or by using a writing program, such as Scrivener (which is my preferred method).

Note: The Premise Formula is outlined for you with each Story Starter topic. The first Story Starter has a premise example (taken from a 1960s cartoon) for you to refer to, if desired.

Have fun!

Scene Number:	Chapter:	Section:

POV Character: **Date:**   **Setting:**

Characters Involved:

Summary of Scene:

Character Goal/Scene Question:

Character Motivation:

Conflict:

Disaster:

Reaction:

Dilemma:

Decision:

Hook:

Items to Research:

STORY STARTER #1

Topic: Automotive

"What if?" Question:

(Situation) When _____

(Protagonist) _____

(Objective) _____

But can he/she _____when

(Opponent) _____

(Climax) _____?

"What if?" Question Example: What if a racecar driver's hopes of winning were thwarted by a dastardly villain, who kidnapped the hero's girlfriend?

Premise Example: When the Thunderbolt Grease-Slapper suffers a blowout and spins out of control, Tom Slick assists mechanic Gertie Growler in the pits so he can return to the track. But can he win the race when Baron Otto Matic kidnaps Slick's girlfriend, Marigold, forcing Tom to choose between winning and rescuing his true love?

Your story notes:

50
VEHICLE
AUTOMOBILE
THIS WAY
SERVICE
OPEN
close
STOP
DRIVE
CAR
AK 1234

STORY STARTER #2

Topic: Camping

"What if?" Question:

(Situation) When _____

(Protagonist) _____

(Objective) _____

But can he/she _____when

(Opponent) _____

(Climax) _____?

Your story notes:

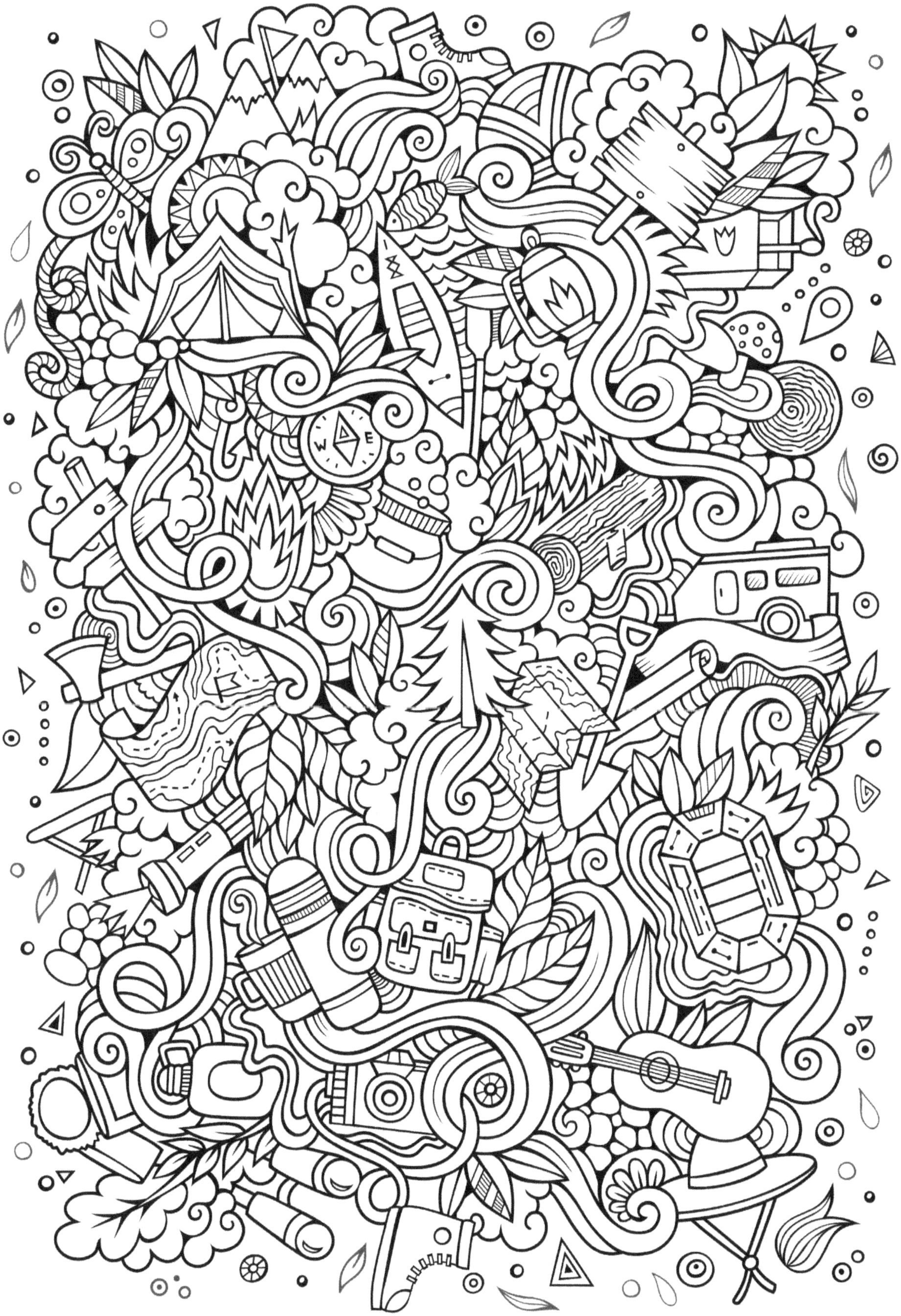

STORY STARTER #3

Topic: Fashion

"What if?" Question:

(Situation) When _____

(Protagonist) _____

(Objective) _____

But can he/she _____when

(Opponent) _____

(Climax) _____?

Your Story Notes:

STORY STARTER #4

Topic: Dieting

"What if?" Question:

(Situation) When _____

(Protagonist) _____

(Objective) _____

But can he/she _____when

(Opponent) _____

(Climax) _____?

Your story notes:

STORY STARTER #5

Topic: Cinema/Theater

"What if?" Question:

(Situation) When _____

(Protagonist) _____

(Objective) _____

But can he/she _____ when

(Opponent) _____

(Climax) _____?

Your story notes:

THE END

MOVIE

CINEMA

OREC

TV

TICKET

PLAY

3D

STORY STARTER #6

Topic: Whodunit

"What if?" Question:

(Situation) When _____

(Protagonist) _____

(Objective) _____

But can he/she _____when

(Opponent) _____

(Climax) _____?

Your story notes:

STORY STARTER #7

Topic: Cosmetics

"What if?" Question:

(Situation) When _____

(Protagonist) _____

(Objective) _____

But can he/she _____ when

(Opponent) _____

(Climax) _____?

Your story notes:

STORY STARTER #8

Topic: Ideas/Brainstorming

"What if?" Question:

(Situation) When _____

(Protagonist) _____

(Objective) _____

But can he/she _____when

(Opponent) _____

(Climax) _____?

Your story notes:

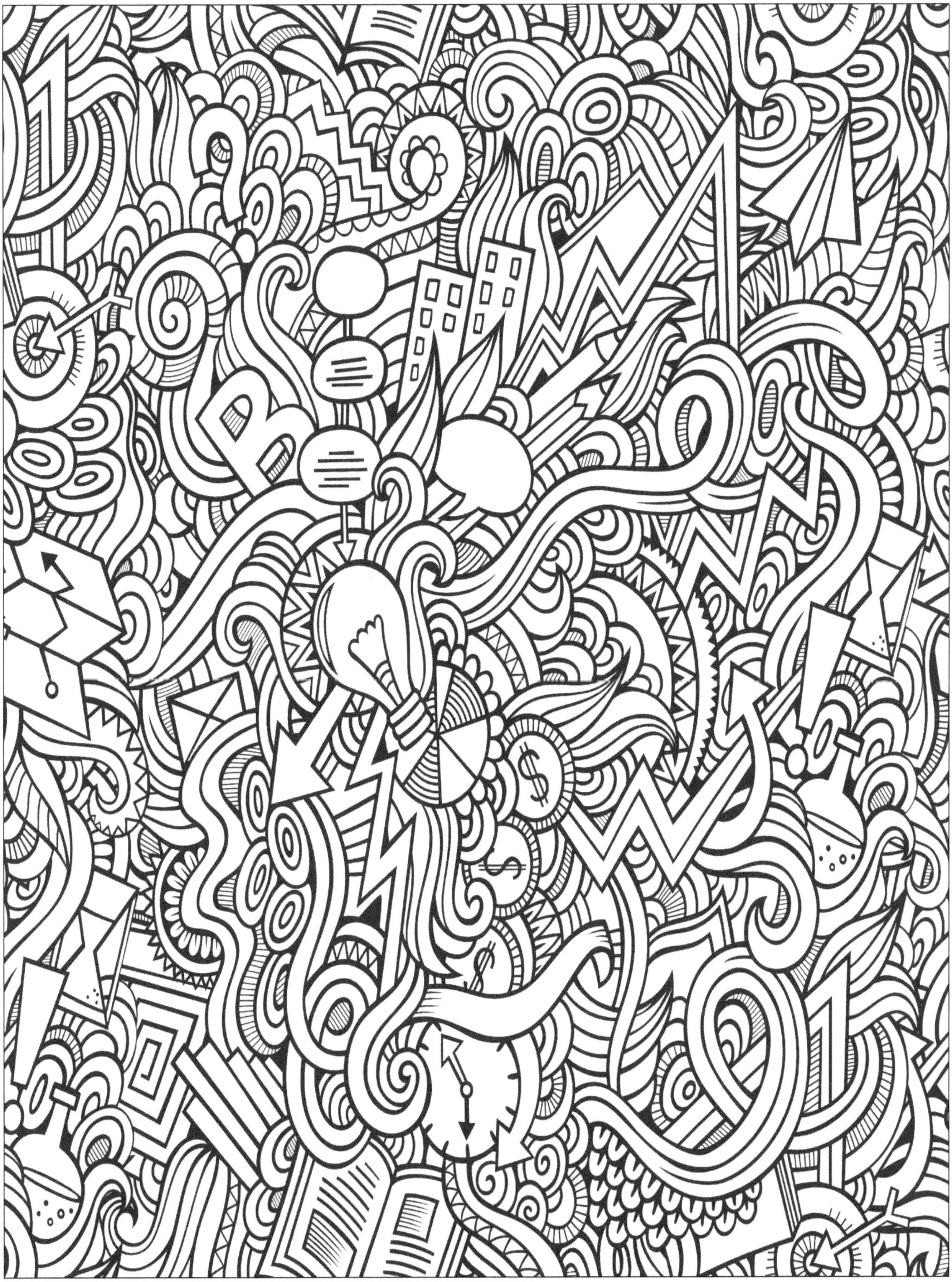

STORY STARTER #9

Topic: Education

"What if?" Question:

(Situation) When _____

(Protagonist) _____

(Objective) _____

But can he/she _____when

(Opponent) _____

(Climax) _____?

Your story notes:

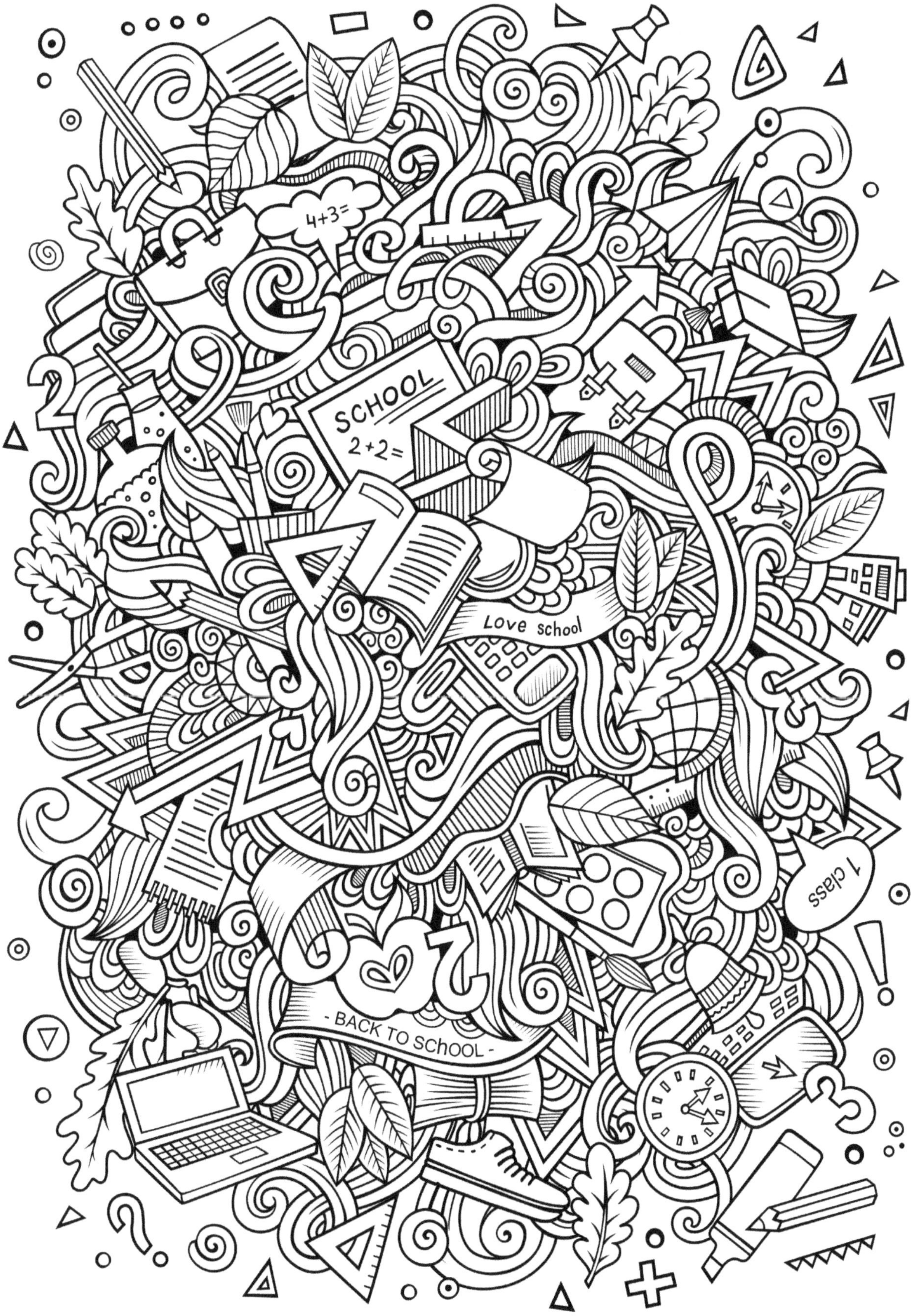
4+3=
SCHOOL
2+2=
Love school
1 class
- BACK TO SCHOOL -

STORY STARTER #10

Topic: Summertime

"What if?" Question:

(Situation) When _____

(Protagonist) _____

(Objective) _____

But can he/she _____ when

(Opponent) _____

(Climax) _____ ?

Your story notes:

STORY STARTER #11

Topic: Springtime

"What if?" Question:

(Situation) When _____

(Protagonist) _____

(Objective) _____

But can he/she _____when

(Opponent) _____

(Climax) _____?

Your story notes:

STORY STARTER #12

Topic: Peas in a Pod

"What if?" Question:

(Situation) When _____

(Protagonist) _____

(Objective) _____

But can he/she _____when

(Opponent) _____

(Climax) _____?

Your story notes:

STORY STARTER #13

Topic: Science

"What if?" Question:

(Situation) When _____

(Protagonist) _____

(Objective) _____

But can he/she _____when

(Opponent) _____

(Climax) _____?

Your story notes:

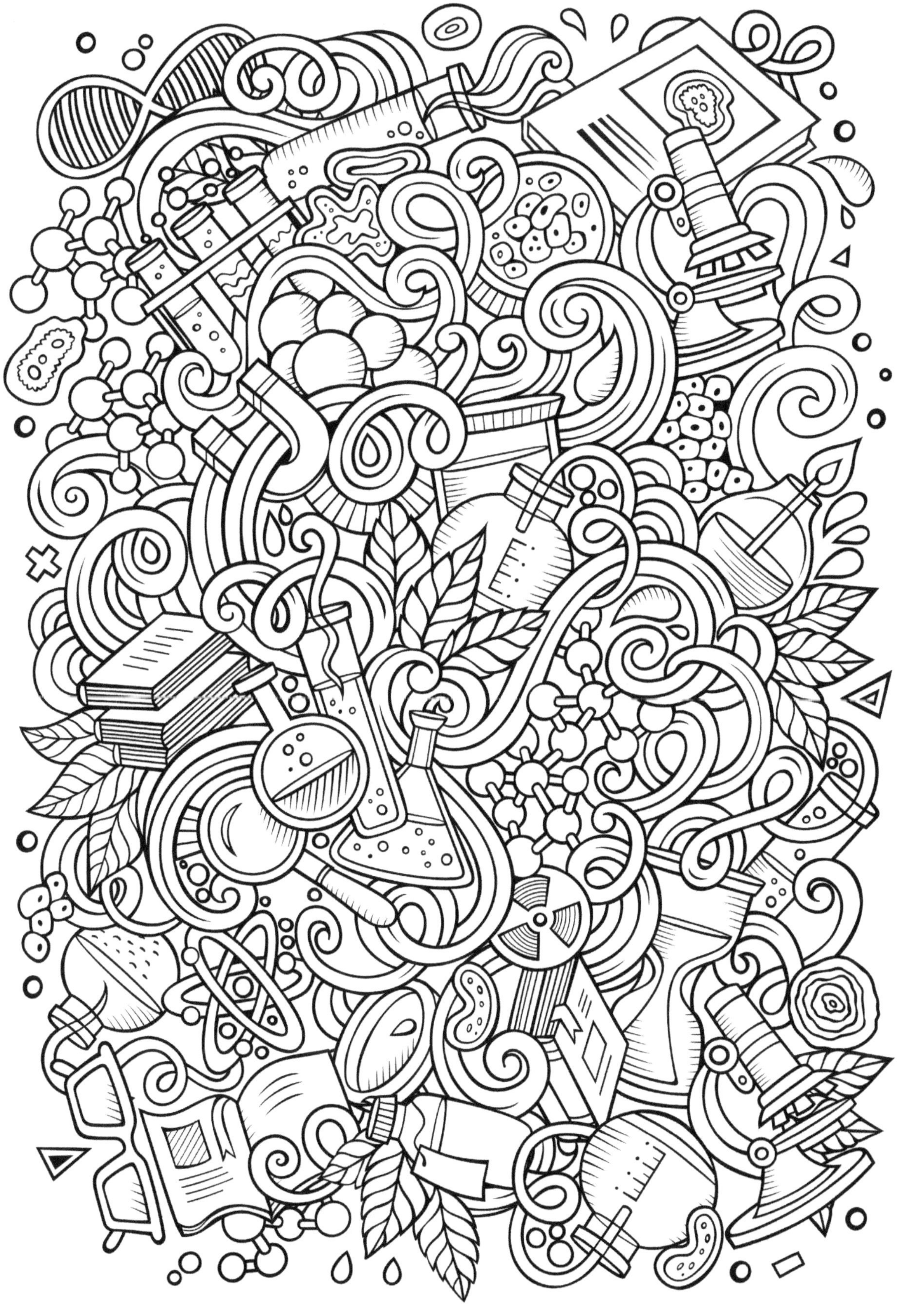

STORY STARTER #14

Topic: Nautical

"What if?" Question:

(Situation) When _____

(Protagonist) _____

(Objective) _____

But can he/she _____when

(Opponent) _____

(Climax) _____?

Your story notes:

STORY STARTER #15

Topic: Internet

"What if?" Question:

(Situation) When _____

(Protagonist) _____

(Objective) _____

But can he/she _____when

(Opponent) _____

(Climax) _____?

Your story notes:

WI-FI
Internet
WI-FI
online
LOGIN
@
http://www.loremipsum.com
http
.com
WWW
share
info
+1
?!!

STORY STARTER #16

Topic: Spa/Massage

"What if?" Question:

(Situation) When _____

(Protagonist) _____

(Objective) _____

But can he/she _____when

(Opponent) _____

(Climax) _____?

Your story notes:

STORY STARTER #17

Topic: Conversation/Communication

"What if?" Question:

(Situation) When _____

(Protagonist) _____

(Objective) _____

But can he/she _____when

(Opponent) _____

(Climax) _____?

Your story notes:

STORY STARTER #18

Topic: Music

"What if?" Question:

(Situation) When _____

(Protagonist) _____

(Objective) _____

But can he/she _____when

(Opponent) _____

(Climax) _____?

Your story notes:

STORY STARTER #19

Topic: Thanksgiving

"What if?" Question:

(Situation) When _____

(Protagonist) _____

(Objective) _____

But can he/she _____when

(Opponent) _____

(Climax) _____?

Your story notes:

THANKSGIVING

26 NOVEMBER

STORY STARTER #20

Topic: Sports

"What if?" Question:

(Situation) When _____

(Protagonist) _____

(Objective) _____

But can he/she _____ when

(Opponent) _____

(Climax) _____ ?

Your story notes:

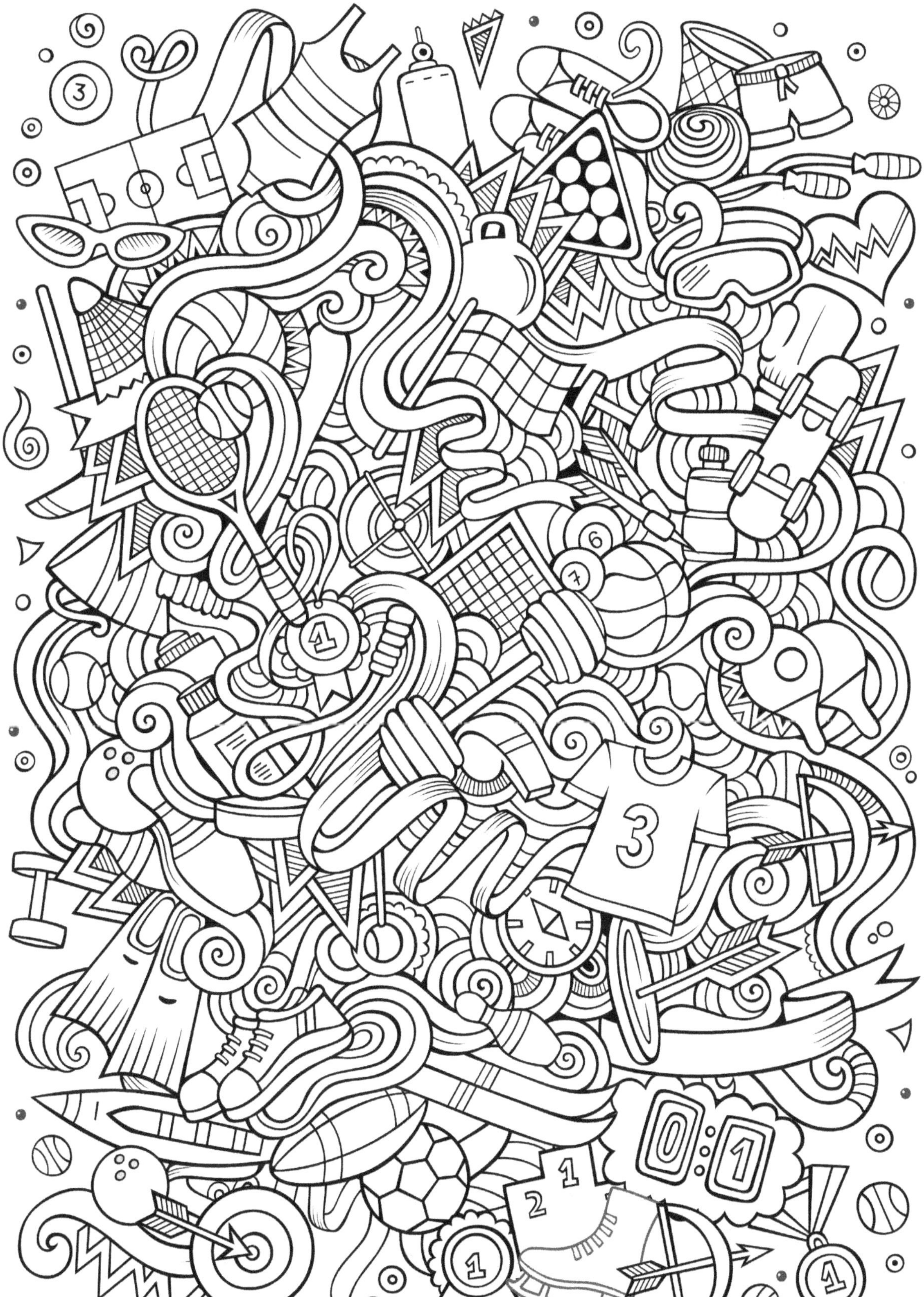

STORY STARTER #21

Topic: Photography

"What if?" Question:

(Situation) When _____

(Protagonist) _____

(Objective) _____

But can he/she _____when

(Opponent) _____

(Climax) _____?

Your story notes:

STORY STARTER #22

Topic: Tea

"What if?" Question:

(Situation) When _____

(Protagonist) _____

(Objective) _____

But can he/she _____when

(Opponent) _____

(Climax) _____?

Your story notes:

STORY STARTER #23

Topic: Texting

"What if?" Question:

(Situation) When _____

(Protagonist) _____

(Objective) _____

But can he/she _____when

(Opponent) _____

(Climax) _____?

Your story notes:

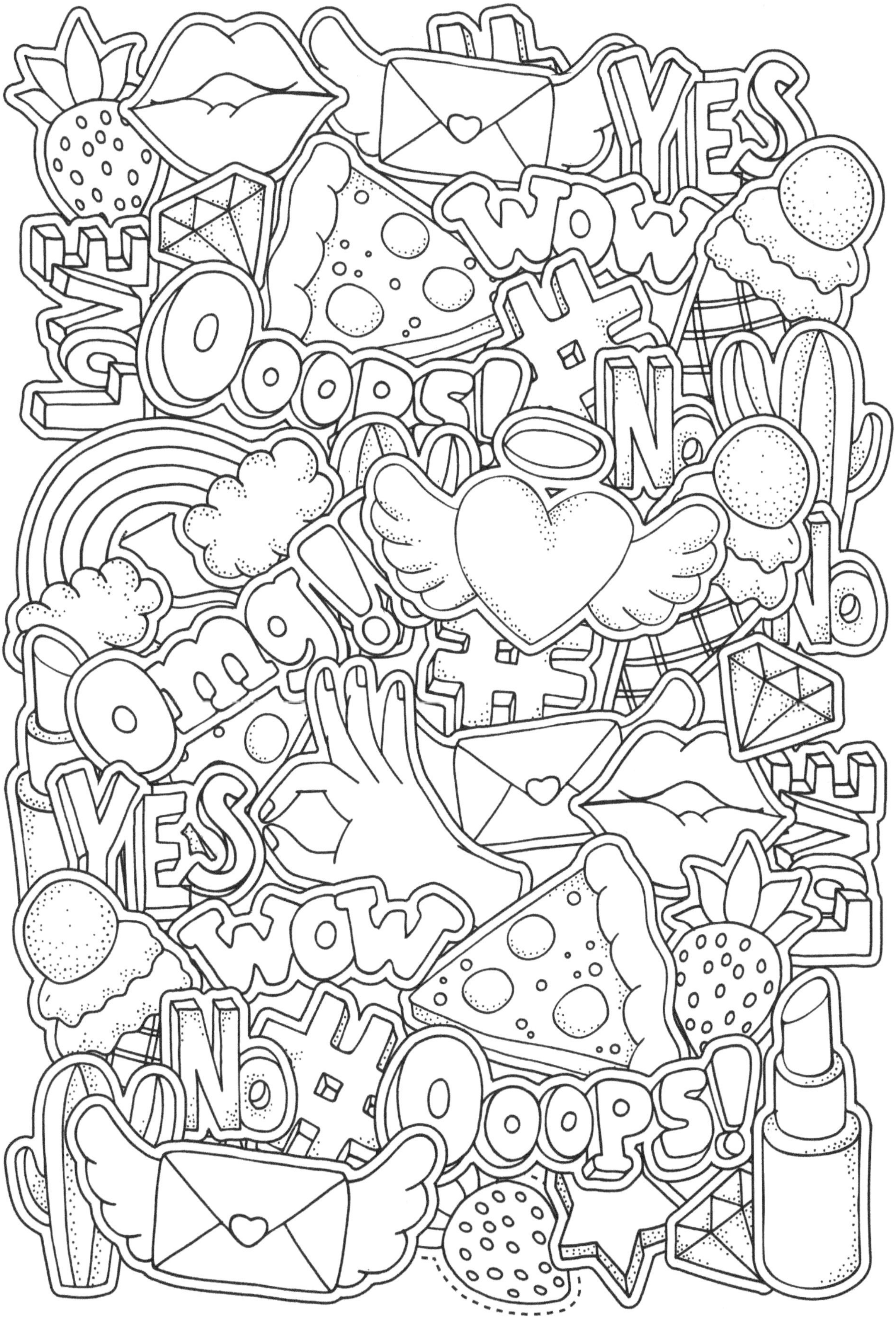
YES
WOW
LOVE
Ooops!
NO
omg!
YES
WOW
LOVE
NO
Ooops!

STORY STARTER #24

Topic: Fish

"What if?" Question:

(Situation) When _____

(Protagonist) _____

(Objective) _____

But can he/she _____ when

(Opponent) _____

(Climax) _____?

Your story notes:

STORY STARTER #25

Topic: Birthday

"What if?" Question:

(Situation) When _____

(Protagonist) _____

(Objective) _____

But can he/she _____when

(Opponent) _____

(Climax) _____?

Your story notes:

BIRTHDAY

STORY STARTER #26

Topic: Shopping

"What if?" Question:

(Situation) When _____

(Protagonist) _____

(Objective) _____

But can he/she _____when

(Opponent) _____

(Climax) _____?

Your story notes:

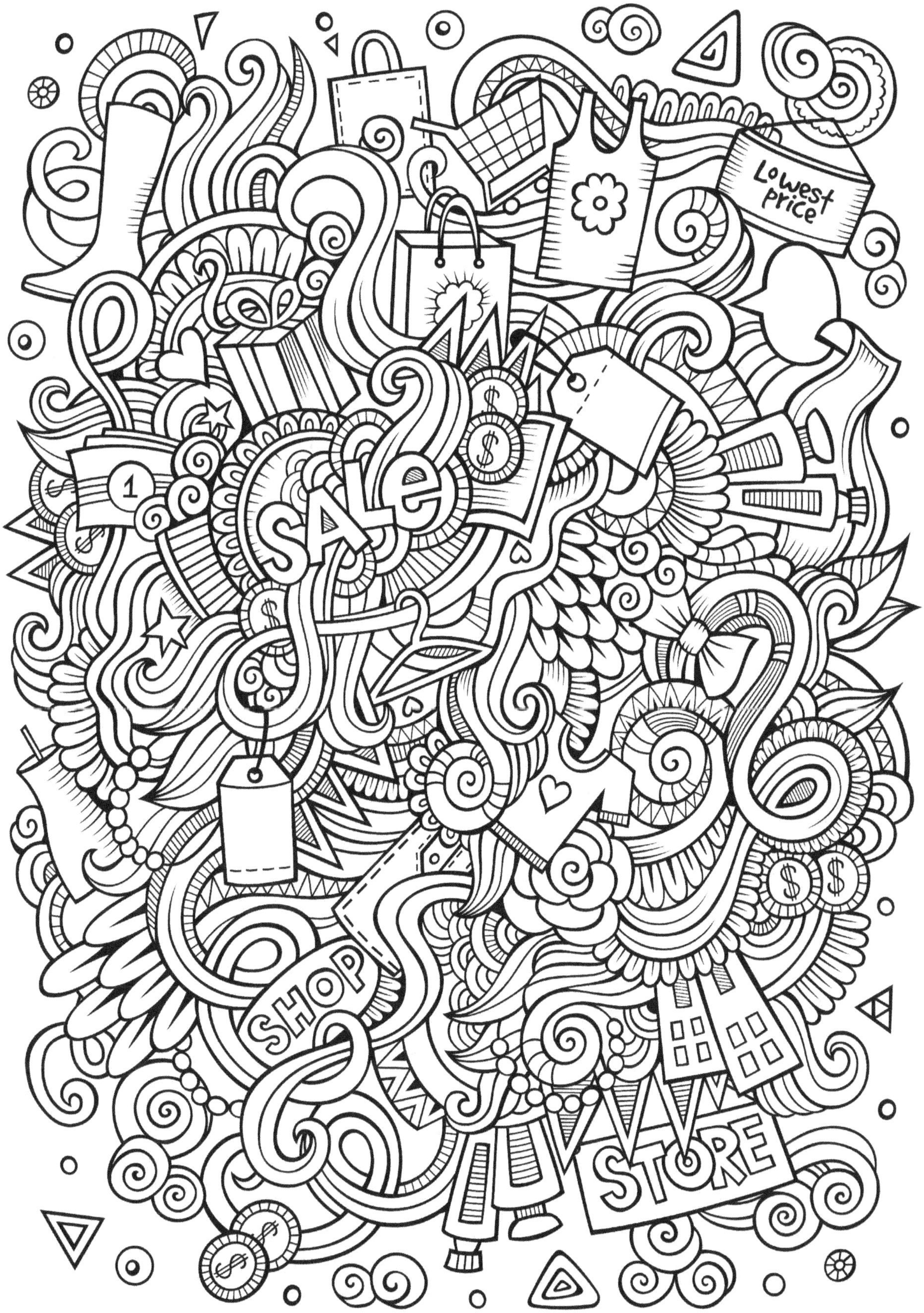
Lowest price
SALE
1
SHOP
STORE

STORY STARTER #27

Topic: Space

"What if?" Question:

(Situation) When _____

(Protagonist) _____

(Objective) _____

But can he/she _____when

(Opponent) _____

(Climax) _____?

Your story notes:

STORY STARTER #28

Topic: Small Town

"What if?" Question:

(Situation) When _____

(Protagonist) _____

(Objective) _____

But can he/she _____ when

(Opponent) _____

(Climax) _____?

Your story notes:

STORY STARTER #29

Topic: Hair Salon

"What if?" Question:

(Situation) When _____

(Protagonist) _____

(Objective) _____

But can he/she _____when

(Opponent) _____

(Climax) _____?

Your story notes:

STORY STARTER #30

Topic: Halloween

"What if?" Question:

(Situation) When _____

(Protagonist) _____

(Objective) _____

But can he/she _____when

(Opponent) _____

(Climax) _____?

Your story notes:

STORY STARTER #31

Topic: India

"What if?" Question:

(Situation) When _____

(Protagonist) _____

(Objective) _____

But can he/she _____when

(Opponent) _____

(Climax) _____?

Your story notes:

STORY STARTER #32

Topic: Africa

"What if?" Question:

(Situation) When _____

(Protagonist) _____

(Objective) _____

But can he/she _____when

(Opponent) _____

(Climax) _____?

Your story notes:

STORY STARTER #33

Topic: Autumn

"What if?" Question:

(Situation) When _____

(Protagonist) _____

(Objective) _____

But can he/she _____when

(Opponent) _____

(Climax) _____?

Your story notes:

STORY STARTER #34

Topic: Bathroom

"What if?" Question:

(Situation) When _____

(Protagonist) _____

(Objective) _____

But can he/she _____when

(Opponent) _____

(Climax) _____?

Your story notes:

STORY STARTER #35

Topic: Sailing

"What if?" Question:

(Situation) When _____

(Protagonist) _____

(Objective) _____

But can he/she _____when

(Opponent) _____

(Climax) _____?

Your story notes:

STORY STARTER #36

Topic: Baby

"What if?" Question:

(Situation) When _____

(Protagonist) _____

(Objective) _____

But can he/she _____ when

(Opponent) _____

(Climax) _____?

Your story notes:

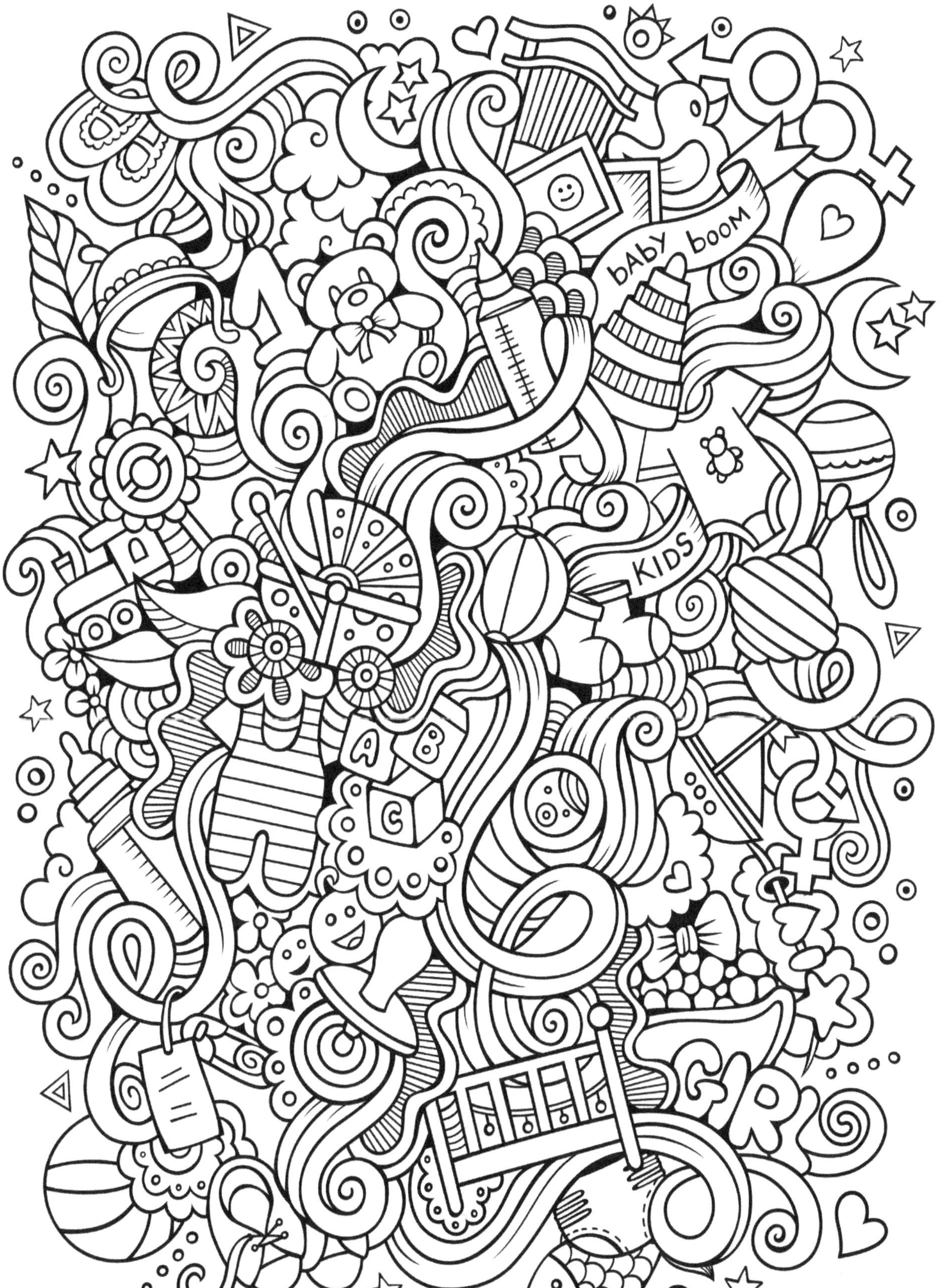
baby boom
KIDS

STORY STARTER #37

Topic: Hippies

"What if?" Question:

(Situation) When _____

(Protagonist) _____

(Objective) _____

But can he/she _____when

(Opponent) _____

(Climax) _____?

Your story notes:

STORY STARTER #38

Topic: Gambling

"What if?" Question:

(Situation) When _____

(Protagonist) _____

(Objective) _____

But can he/she _____when

(Opponent) _____

(Climax) _____?

Your story notes:

STORY STARTER #39

Topic: Honey

"What if?" Question:

(Situation) When _____

(Protagonist) _____

(Objective) _____

But can he/she _____when

(Opponent) _____

(Climax) _____?

Your story notes:

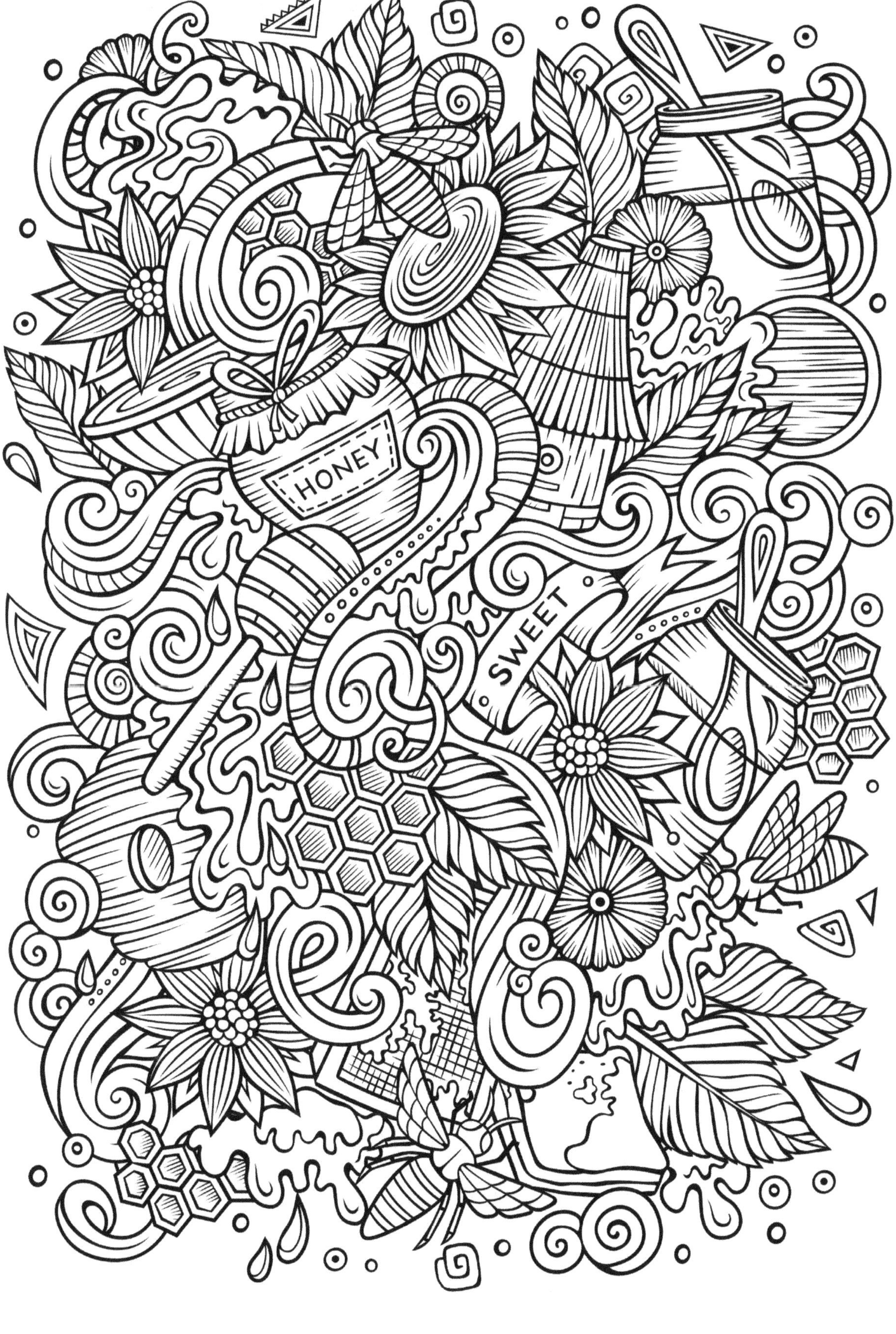
HONEY
SWEET

STORY STARTER #40

Topic: Plants

"What if?" Question:

(Situation) When _____

(Protagonist) _____

(Objective) _____

But can he/she _____when

(Opponent) _____

(Climax) _____?

Your story notes:

STORY STARTER #41

Topic: Disco

"What if?" Question:

(Situation) When _____

(Protagonist) _____

(Objective) _____

But can he/she _____when

(Opponent) _____

(Climax) _____?

Your story notes:

STORY STARTER #42

Topic: Health

"What if?" Question:

(Situation) When _____

(Protagonist) _____

(Objective) _____

But can he/she _____when

(Opponent) _____

(Climax) _____?

Your story notes:

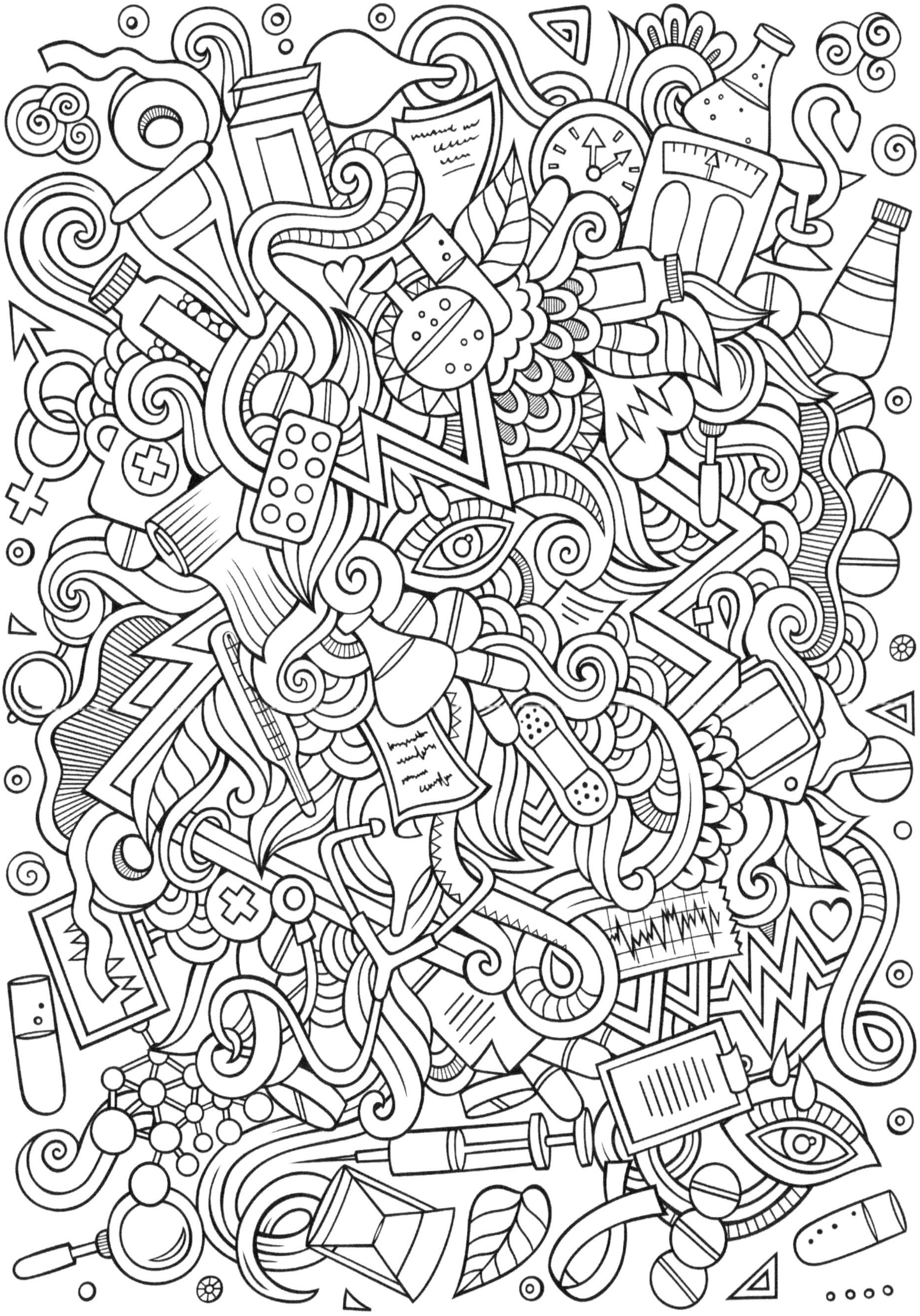

STORY STARTER #43

Topic: Travel

"What if?" Question:

(Situation) When _____

(Protagonist) _____

(Objective) _____

But can he/she _____when

(Opponent) _____

(Climax) _____?

Your story notes:

STORY STARTER #44

Topic: Sea Life

"What if?" Question:

(Situation) When _____

(Protagonist) _____

(Objective) _____

But can he/she _____when

(Opponent) _____

(Climax) _____?

Your story notes:

STORY STARTER #45

Topic: Germany

"What if?" Question:

(Situation) When _____

(Protagonist) _____

(Objective) _____

But can he/she _____when

(Opponent) _____

(Climax) _____?

Your story notes:

STORY STARTER #46

Topic: Big City

"What if?" Question:

(Situation) When _____

(Protagonist) _____

(Objective) _____

But can he/she _____when

(Opponent) _____

(Climax) _____?

Your story notes:.

STORY STARTER #47

Topic: Junk Food

"What if?" Question:

(Situation) When _____

(Protagonist) _____

(Objective) _____

But can he/she _____when

(Opponent) _____

(Climax) _____?

Your story notes:

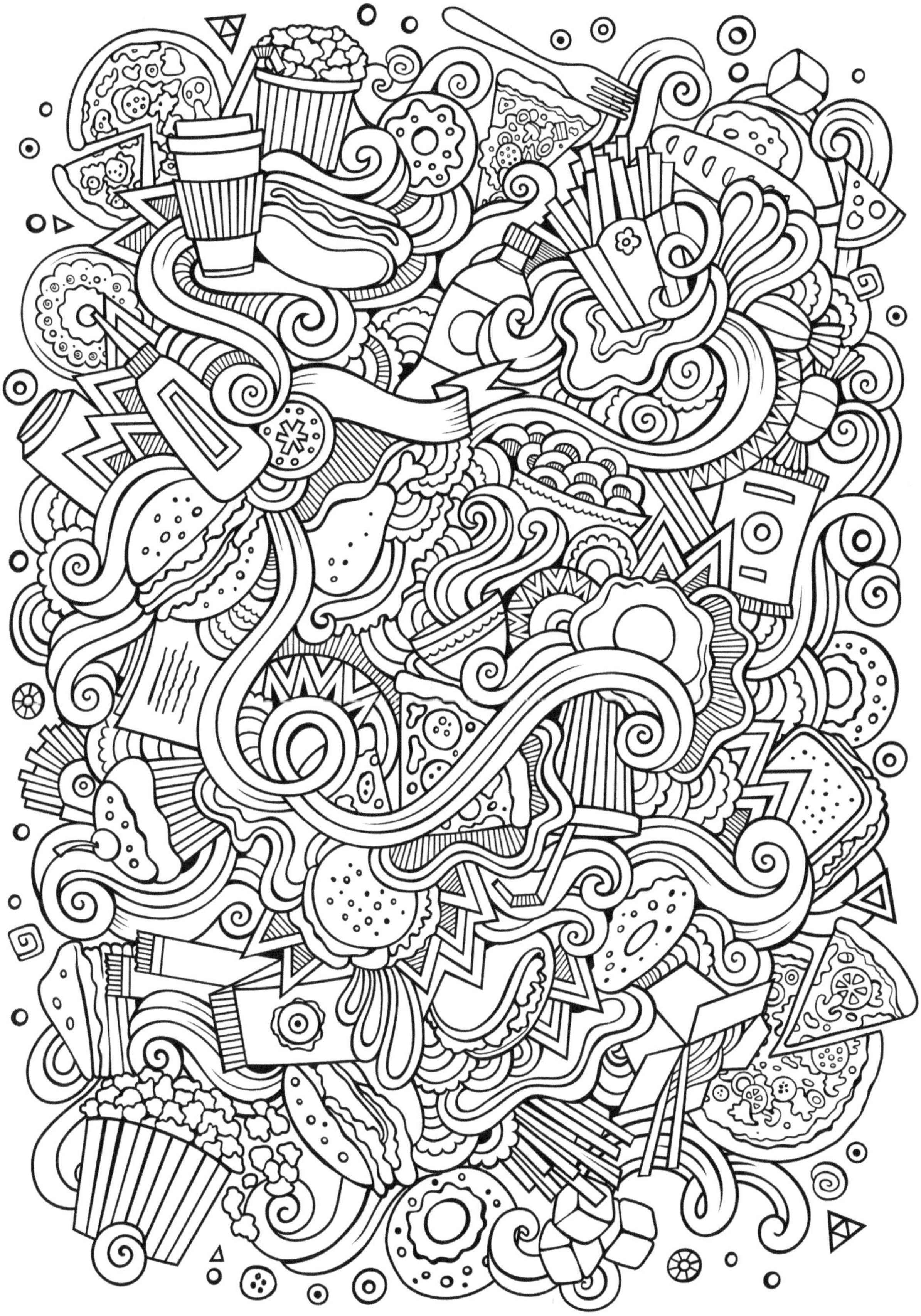

STORY STARTER #48

Topic: Christmas/New Year's

"What if?" Question:

(Situation) When _____

(Protagonist) _____

(Objective) _____

But can he/she _____when

(Opponent) _____

(Climax) _____?

Your story notes:

STORY STARTER #49

Topic: Wedding

"What if?" Question:

(Situation) When _____

(Protagonist) _____

(Objective) _____

But can he/she _____when

(Opponent) _____

(Climax) _____?

Your story notes:

STORY STARTER #50

Topic: Letters/Words

"What if?" Question:

(Situation) When _____

(Protagonist) _____

(Objective) _____

But can he/she _____when

(Opponent) _____

(Climax) _____?

Your story notes:

STORY STARTER #51

Topic: Coffee

"What if?" Question:

(Situation) When _____

(Protagonist) _____

(Objective) _____

But can he/she _____when

(Opponent) _____

(Climax) _____?

Your story notes:

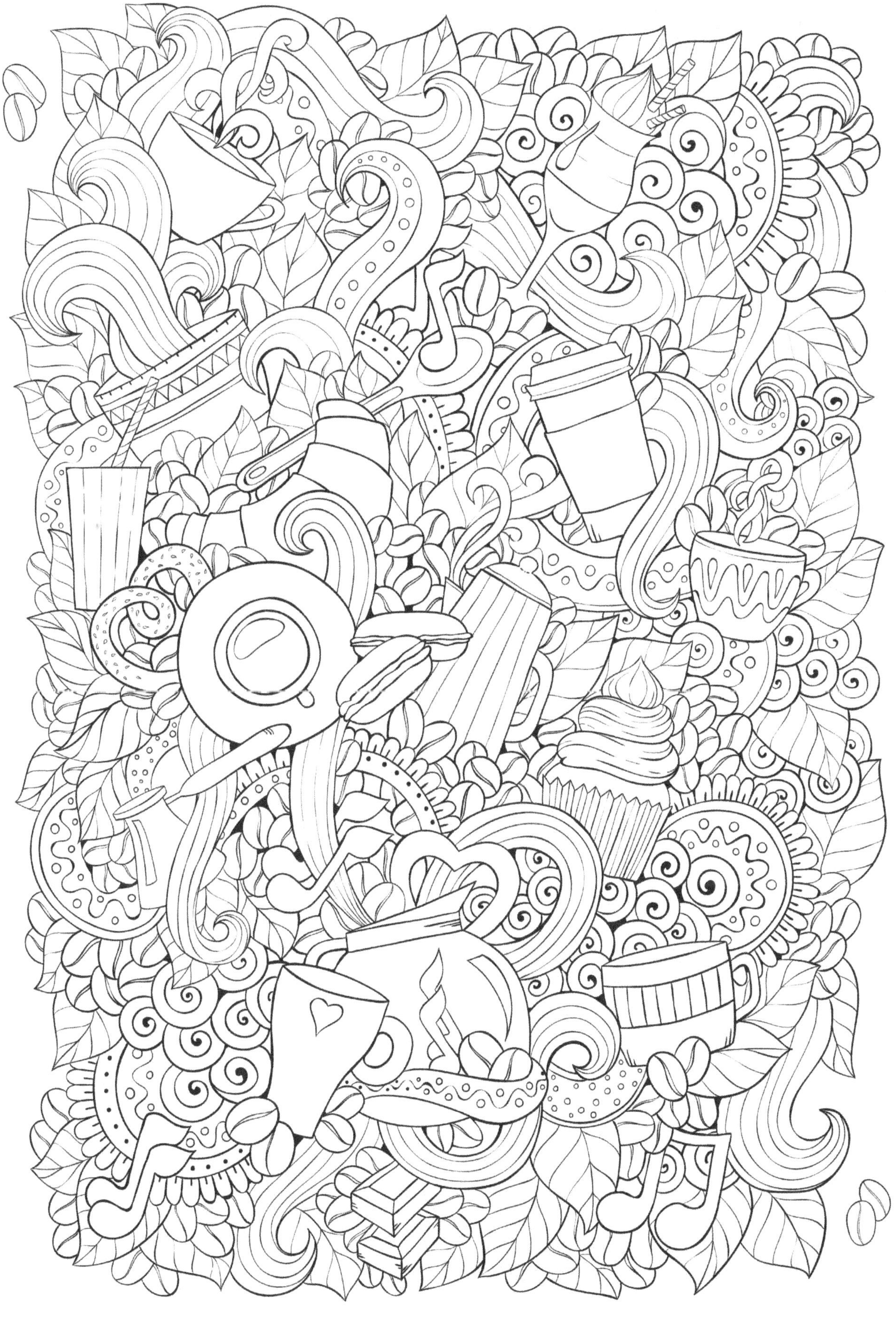

STORY STARTER #52

Topic: Sunrise

"What if?" Question:

(Situation) When _____

(Protagonist) _____

(Objective) _____

But can he/she _____ when

(Opponent) _____

(Climax) _____ ?

Your story notes:

STORY STARTER #53

Topic: Easter

"What if?" Question:

(Situation) When _____

(Protagonist) _____

(Objective) _____

But can he/she _____when

(Opponent) _____

(Climax) _____?

Your story notes:

STORY STARTER #54

Topic: Cookout/Picnic

"What if?" Question:

(Situation) When _____

(Protagonist) _____

(Objective) _____

But can he/she _____when

(Opponent) _____

(Climax) _____?

Your story notes:

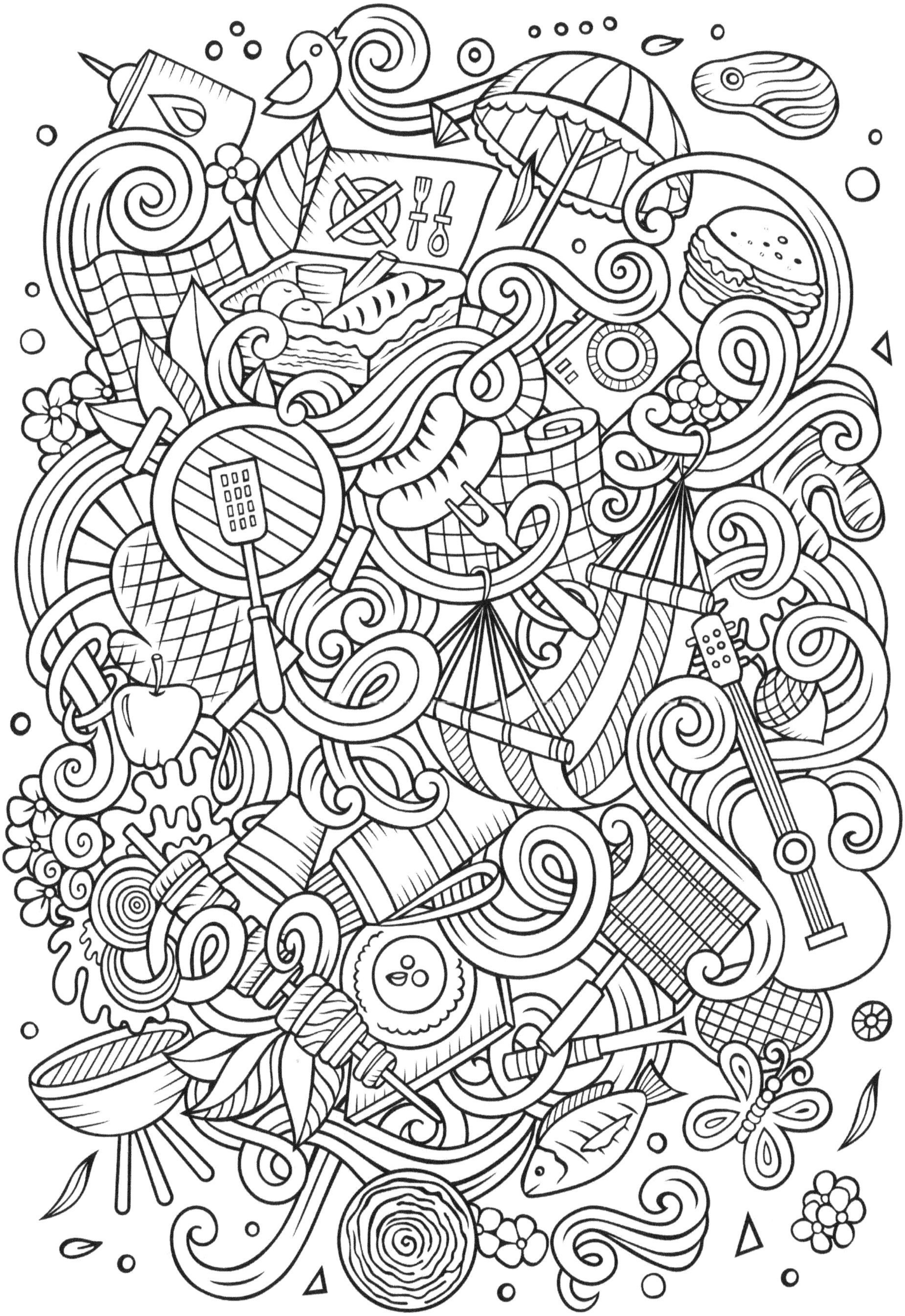

STORY STARTER #55

Topic: Handcrafts

"What if?" Question:

(Situation) When _____

(Protagonist) _____

(Objective) _____

But can he/she _____when

(Opponent) _____

(Climax) _____?

Your story notes:

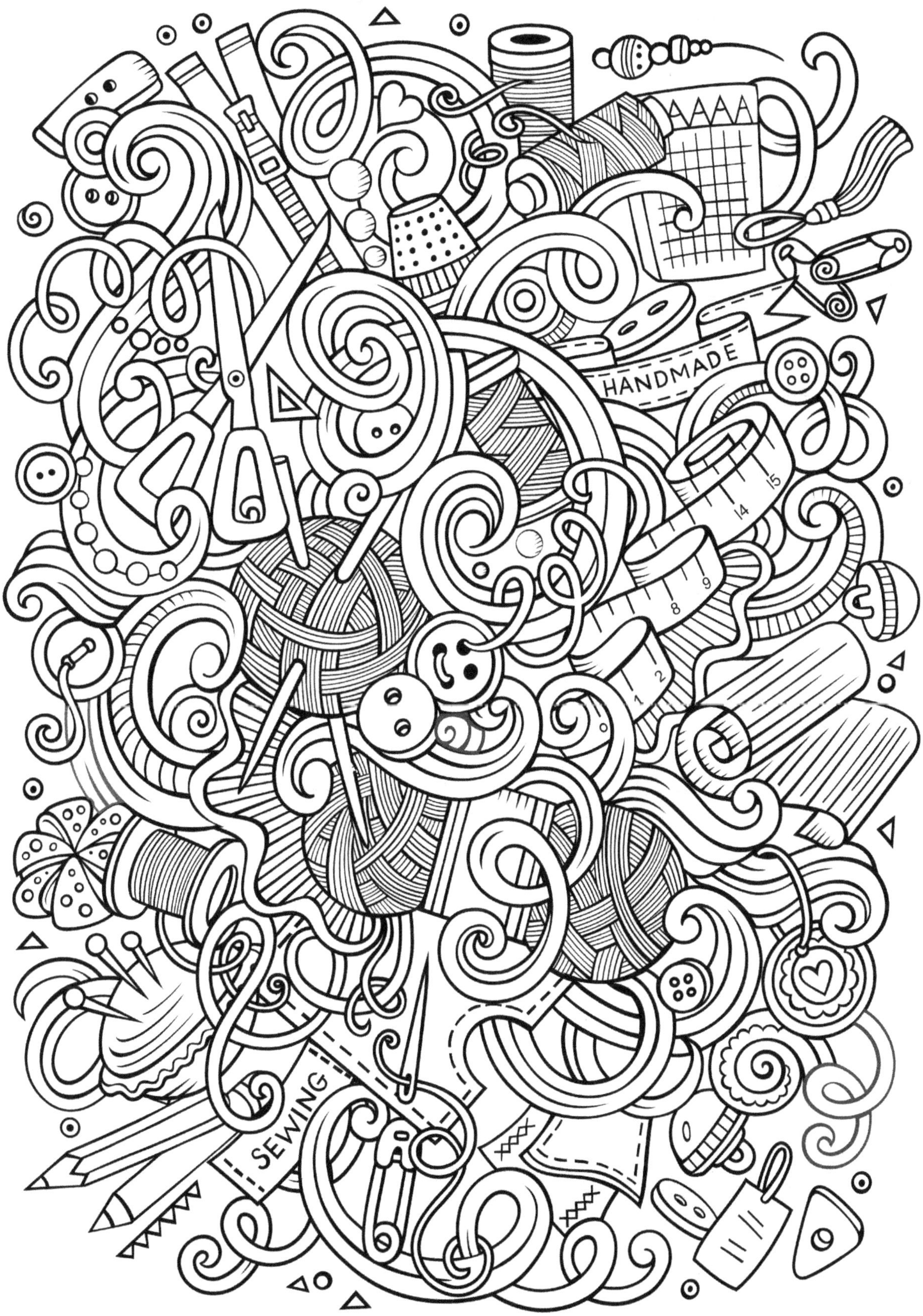
HANDMADE
SEWING

STORY STARTER #56

Topic: Italian Food

"What if?" Question:

(Situation) When _____

(Protagonist) _____

(Objective) _____

But can he/she _____when

(Opponent) _____

(Climax) _____?

Your story notes:

STORY STARTER #57

Topic: Art/Graphic Design

"What if?" Question:

(Situation) When _____

(Protagonist) _____

(Objective) _____

But can he/she _____when

(Opponent) _____

(Climax) _____?

Your story notes:

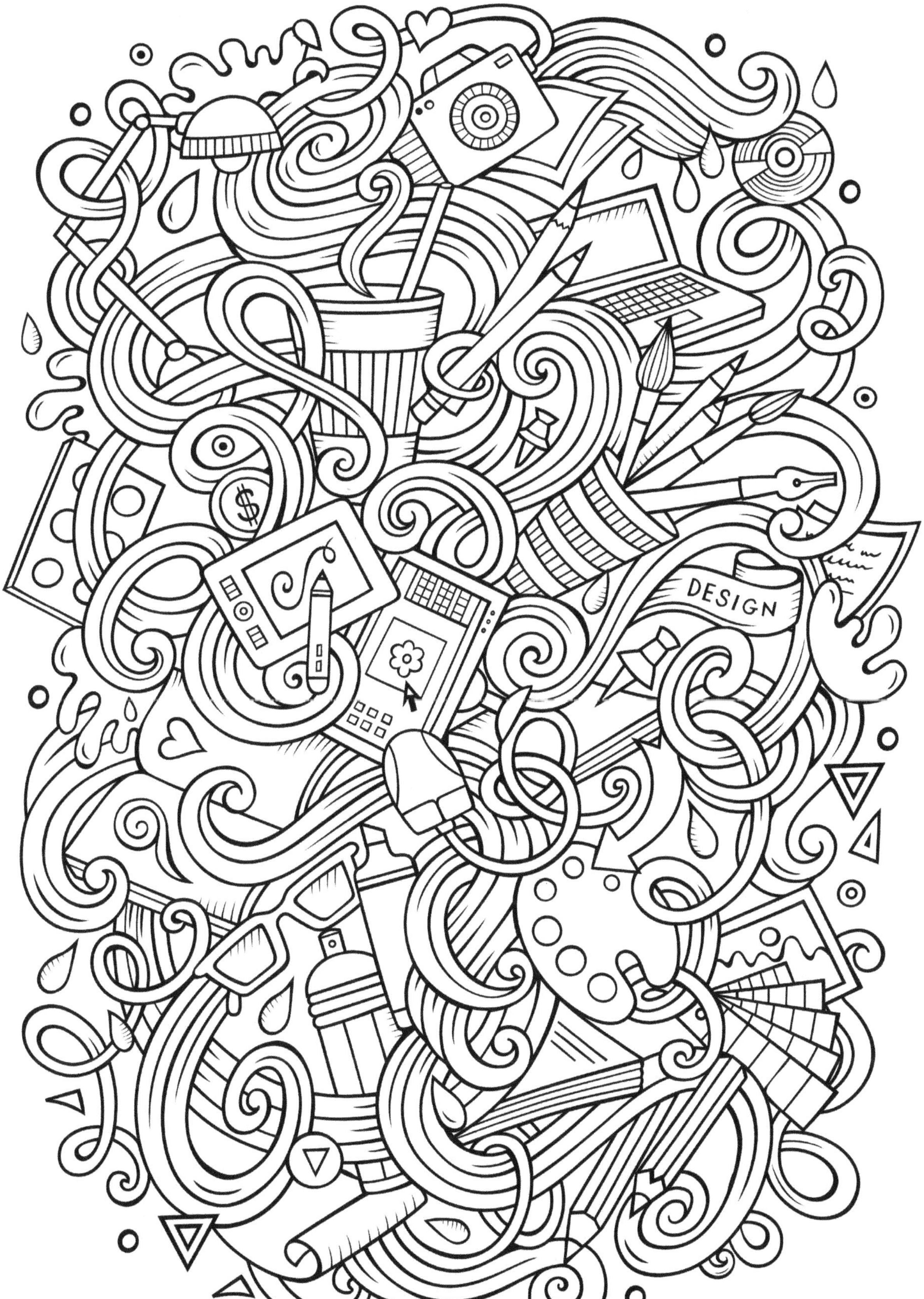
DESIGN

STORY STARTER #58

Topic: Path through the Woods

"What if?" Question:

(Situation) When _____

(Protagonist) _____

(Objective) _____

But can he/she _____when

(Opponent) _____

(Climax) _____?

Your story notes:

STORY STARTER #59

Topic: Mexico

"What if?" Question:

(Situation) When _____

(Protagonist) _____

(Objective) _____

But can he/she _____when

(Opponent) _____

(Climax) _____?

Your story notes:

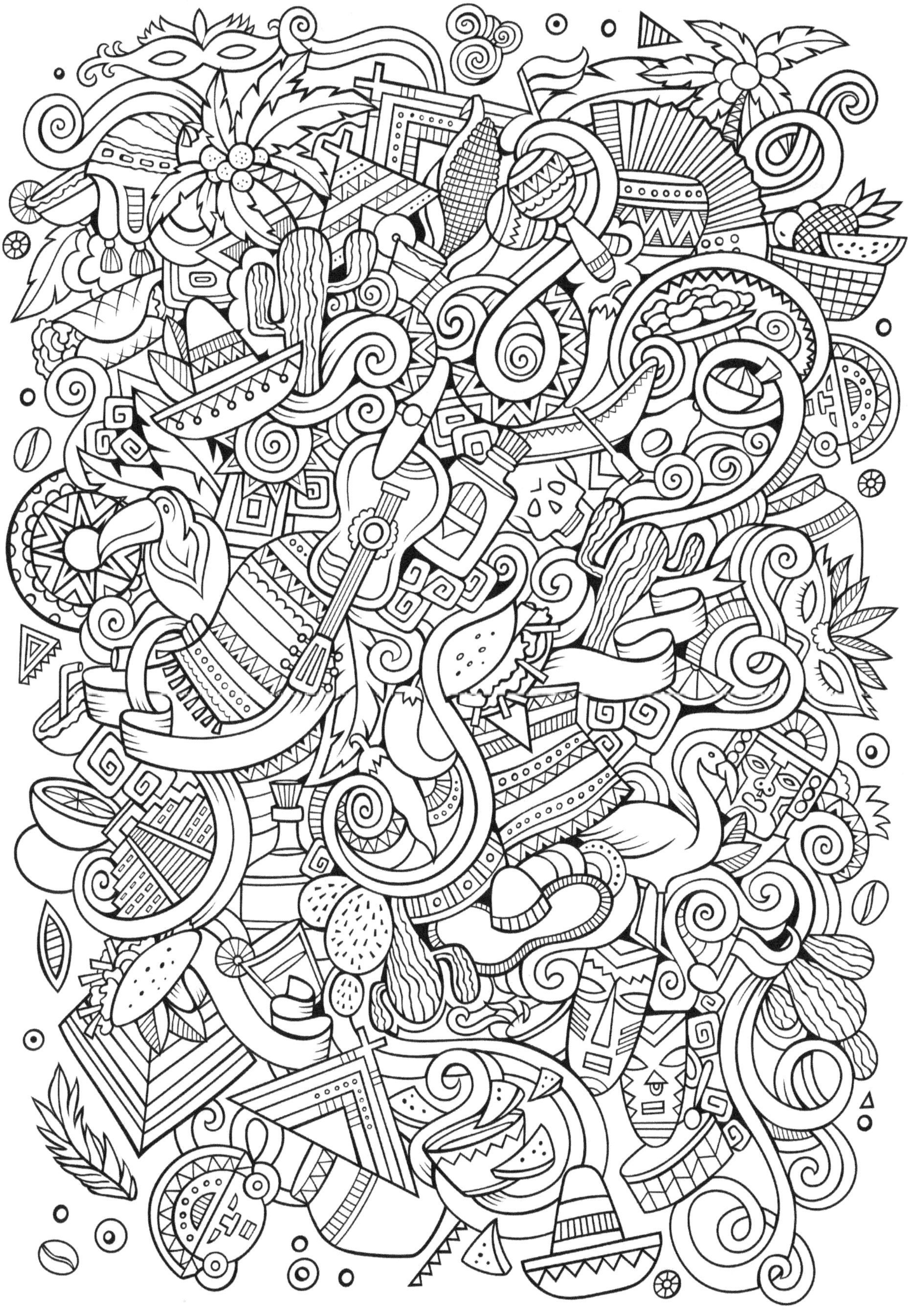

STORY STARTER #60

Topic: Love

"What if?" Question:

(Situation) When _____

(Protagonist) _____

(Objective) _____

But can he/she _____when

(Opponent) _____

(Climax) _____?

Your story notes:

STORY STARTER #61

Topic: Economy Cars

"What if?" Question:

(Situation) When _____

(Protagonist) _____

(Objective) _____

But can he/she _____when

(Opponent) _____

(Climax) _____?

Your story notes:

ELECTRIC

EV

STORY STARTER #62

Topic: Soccer

"What if?" Question:

(Situation) When _____

(Protagonist) _____

(Objective) _____

But can he/she _____ when

(Opponent) _____

(Climax) _____ ?

Your story notes:

STORY STARTER #63

Topic: Nail Salon

"What if?" Question:

(Situation) When _____

(Protagonist) _____

(Objective) _____

But can he/she _____when

(Opponent) _____

(Climax) _____?

Your story notes:

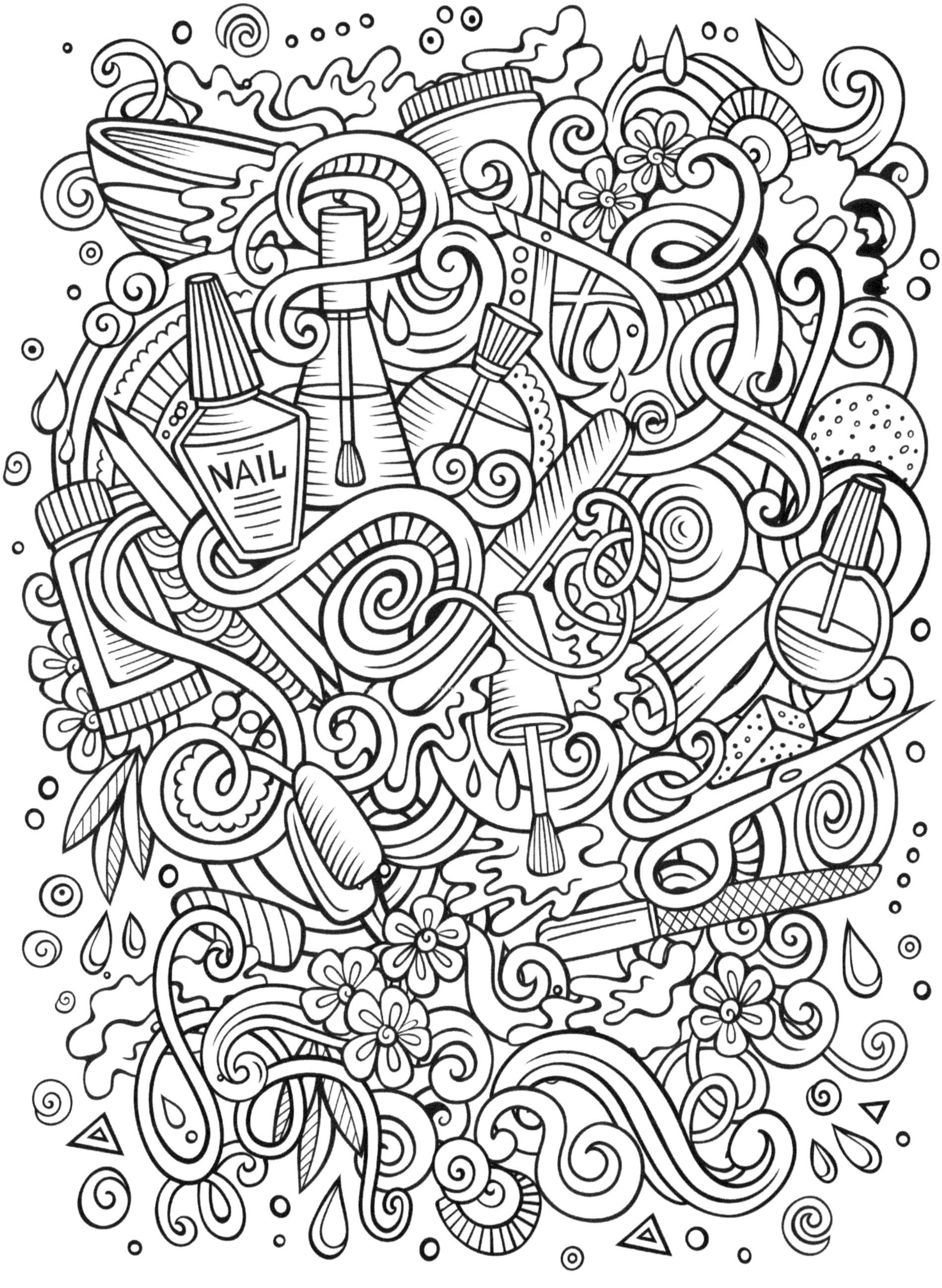
NAIL

STORY STARTER #64

Topic: Automotive

"What if?" Question:

(Situation) When _____

(Protagonist) _____

(Objective) _____

But can he/she _____when

(Opponent) _____

(Climax) _____?

Your story notes:

STORY STARTER #65

Topic: Tents and Trees

"What if?" Question:

(Situation) When _____

(Protagonist) _____

(Objective) _____

But can he/she _____ when

(Opponent) _____

(Climax) _____ ?

Your story notes:

STORY STARTER #66

Topic: Broken Hearts

"What if?" Question:

(Situation) When _____

(Protagonist) _____

(Objective) _____

But can he/she _____when

(Opponent) _____

(Climax) _____?

Your story notes:

STORY STARTER #67

Topic: Sea Shells

"What if?" Question:

(Situation) When _____

(Protagonist) _____

(Objective) _____

But can he/she _____when

(Opponent) _____

(Climax) _____?

Your story notes:

STORY STARTER #68

Topic: Drive through the Countryside

"What if?" Question:

(Situation) When _____

(Protagonist) _____

(Objective) _____

But can he/she _____ when

(Opponent) _____

(Climax) _____ ?

Your story notes:

STORY STARTER #69

Topic: Canning Jars

"What if?" Question:

(Situation) When _____

(Protagonist) _____

(Objective) _____

But can he/she _____when

(Opponent) _____

(Climax) _____?

Your story notes:

STORY STARTER #70

Topic: Ice Cream

"What if?" Question:

(Situation) When _____

(Protagonist) _____

(Objective) _____

But can he/she _____when

(Opponent) _____

(Climax) _____?

Your story notes:

STORY STARTER #71

Topic: Japanese Food

"What if?" Question:

(Situation) When _____

(Protagonist) _____

(Objective) _____

But can he/she _____ when

(Opponent) _____

(Climax) _____ ?

Your story notes:

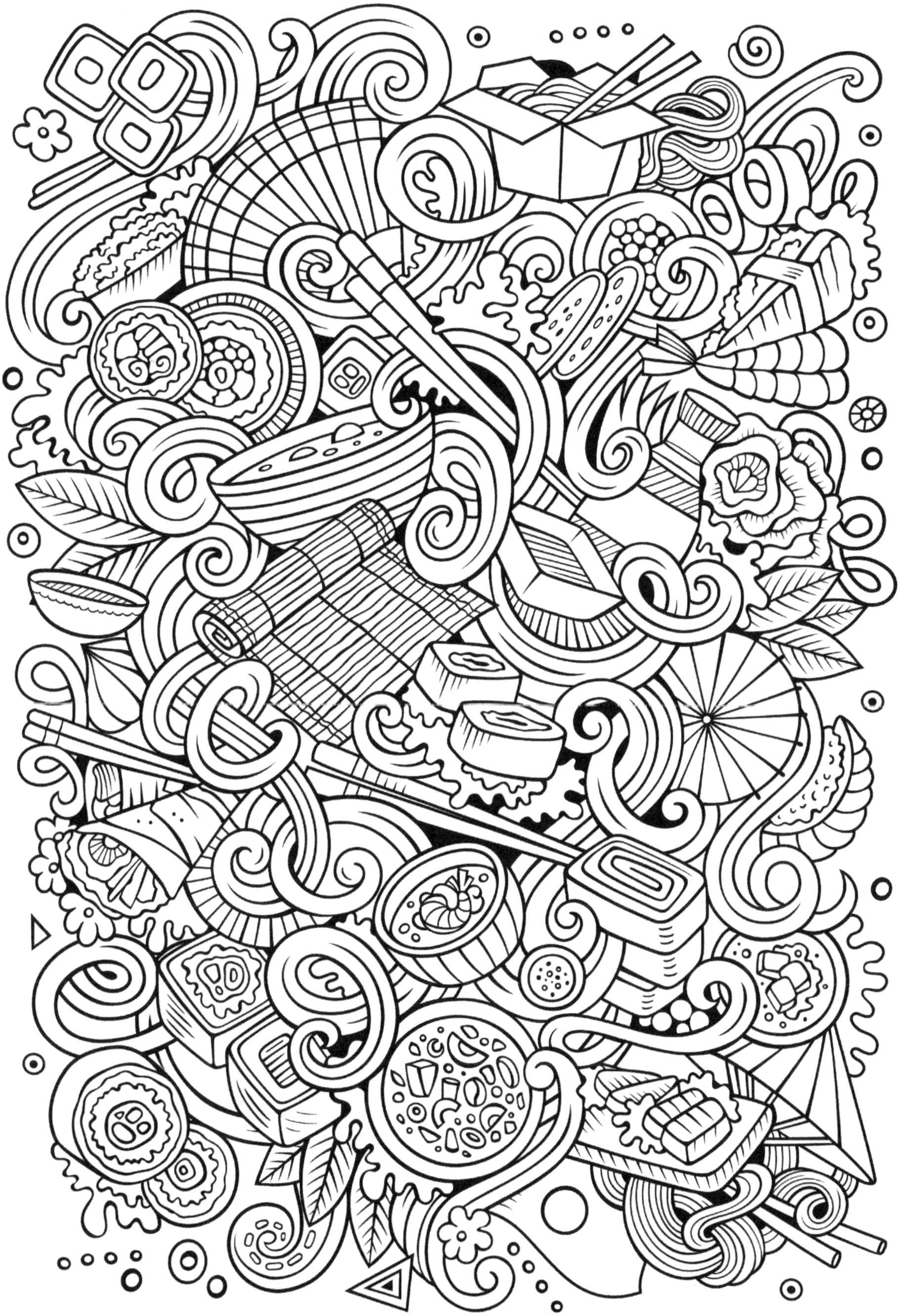

STORY STARTER #72

Topic: Pencils/Writing

"What if?" Question:

(Situation) When _____

(Protagonist) _____

(Objective) _____

But can he/she _____when

(Opponent) _____

(Climax) _____?

Your story notes:

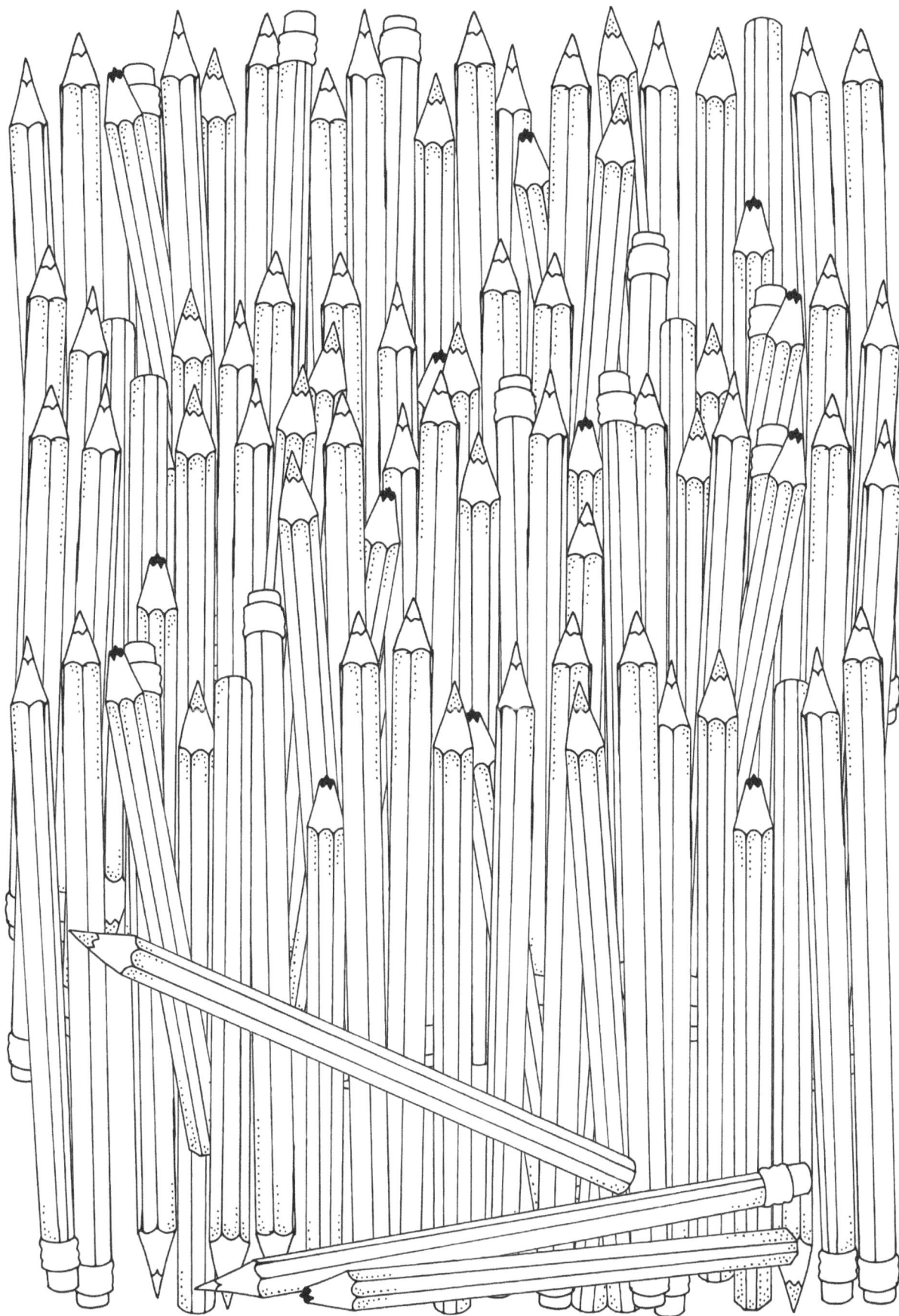

STORY STARTER #73

Topic: Mountains

"What if?" Question:

(Situation) When _____

(Protagonist) _____

(Objective) _____

But can he/she _____ when

(Opponent) _____

(Climax) _____?

Your story notes:

STORY STARTER #74

Topic: Technology

"What if?" Question:

(Situation) When _____

(Protagonist) _____

(Objective) _____

But can he/she _____when

(Opponent) _____

(Climax) _____?

Your story notes:

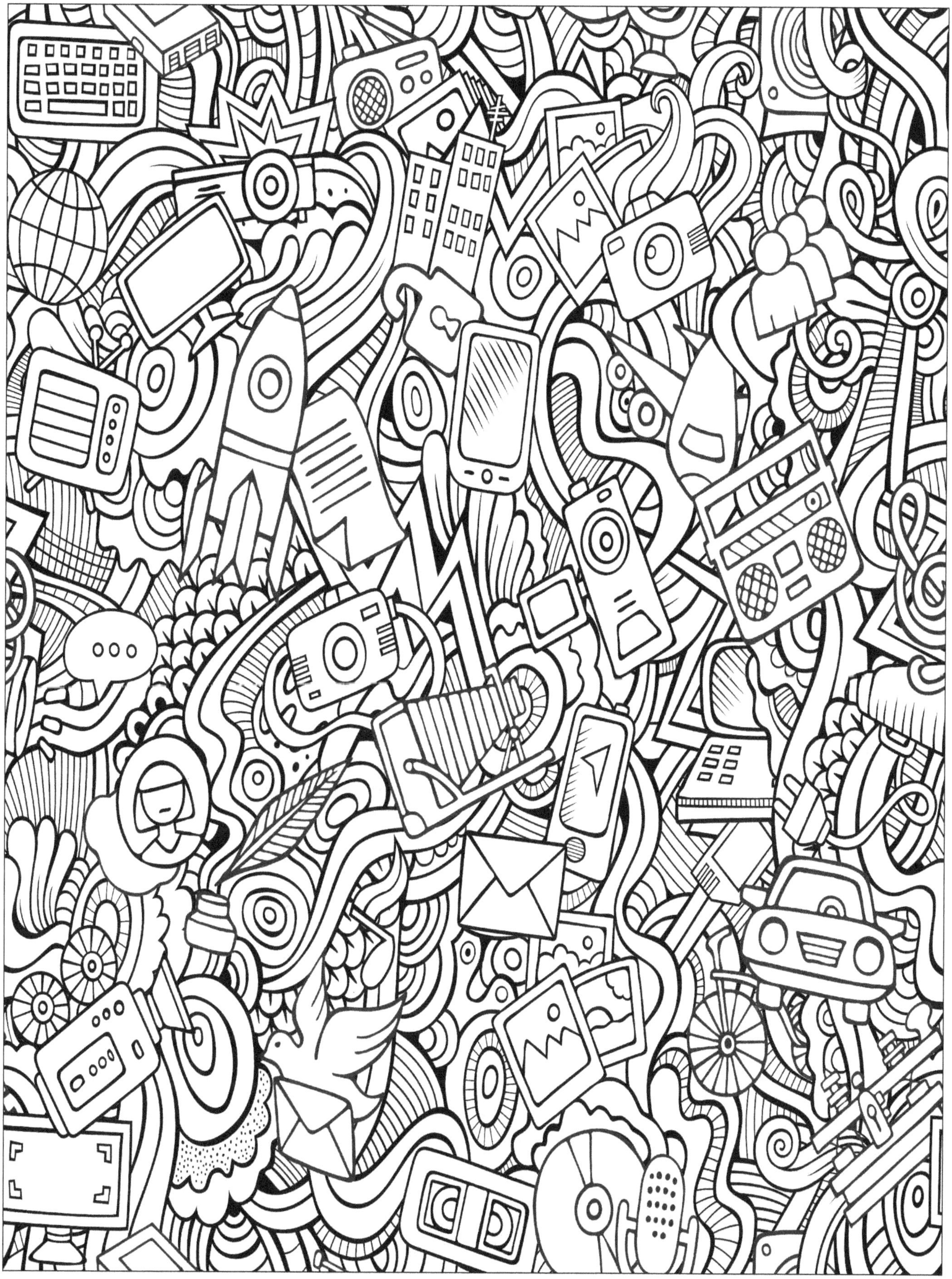

STORY STARTER #75

Topic: House

"What if?" Question:

(Situation) When _____

(Protagonist) _____

(Objective) _____

But can he/she _____when

(Opponent) _____

(Climax) _____?

Your story notes:

OTHER BOOKS BY LINDA FULKERSON

Fiction

Dead Broke (River Valley Mysteries Book 1)

Wings of the Dawn

Coloring Books

The Coloring Book for Writers Volume I

The Coloring Book for Writers Volume II

Coloring Books for Writers: Coffee Lover's Edition

Nonfiction

Ordinary Girl, Extraordinary Purpose: Life Lessons from the Book of Esther

The Habit-Driven Writer (Motivation for Writers Series Book 2)

Mastering the Power of Momentum (Motivation for Writers Series Book 1)

Mastering Memory

The Prodigal Daughter: Hope for Runaway Christians and Those Who Await Their Return

To learn more about these books, please visit my author page at Amazon:

www.amazon.com/author/lindanixonfulkerson

ABOUT LINDA FULKERSON

Linda Fulkerson is the author of *The Prodigal Daughter: Hope for Runaway Christians and Those Who Await Their Return* (2003, Petit Jean Press), and has two novels, *Wings of the Dawn* (historical romance), and *Dead Broke* (mystery), available in both paperback and for Kindle at Amazon.com.

She has also written several marketing-related books and eBooks and published Volumes I and II of *The Coloring Book for Writers* (available at Amazon.com and CreateSpace.com).

Linda is a blog and marketing coach, award-winning photographer, and is the former online editor and director of digital services for the *Killeen Daily Herald*. She is also a former sports writer for the *Petit Jean Country Headlight*.

Linda is a past finalist in the American Christian Fiction Writers (ACFW) Genesis contest, taking second-place in the Young Adult category, and served as ACFW Arkansas Area Coordinator for four years. She is a CLASSeminar graduate and conducts workshops on blogging, marketing, website development, and self-publishing.

Linda is the owner of DLF Digital Services LLC in Morrilton, Arkansas. She and her husband, Don, have four adult children and eight grandchildren. They live in central Arkansas.

www.ingramcontent.com/pod-product-compliance
Lightning Source LLC
Chambersburg PA
CBHW081655270326
41933CB00017B/3177